BENDING UNDER THE
YELLOW POLICE TAPES

STEEL
TOE
BOOKS

BENDING UNDER THE YELLOW POLICE TAPES

JAMES DOYLE

STEEL
TOE
BOOKS

BOWLING GREEN, KENTUCKY

Book Design by Jill Ihasz
Cover Art and Design by C. L. Knight

Steel Toe Books
Department of English
Western Kentucky University
1906 College Heights Blvd. #11086
Bowling Green, KY 42101-1086.
www.steeltoebooks.com

CONTENTS

ACKNOWLEDGEMENTS

Alaska Quarterly Review: "Exile in Japan"
The Alembic: "The Catacombs in Rome"
Apalachee Review: "Desert Motel"
Birmingham Poetry Review: "In the Pasture"
Blue Mesa Review: "No Introductions Necessary"
The Briar Cliff Review: "The Blackberries"
    and "The Tower of Babel"
Cimarron Review: "In Cuzco"
Connecticut Review: "On the Widow's Walk"
Denver Quarterly: "Marco Polo"
descant: "Cracked Lips"
88: "Going from the Paintings to the Desert"
The Florida Review: "The Blue Dress"
The Green Hills Literary Lantern: "Hands at Seventy"
    and "In the Wine Country of Spain"
Gulf Coast: "The Elephant Burial Ground"
Karamu: "The List"
Laurel Review: "Vitamins"
Lilies and Cannonballs Review: "I Found Two Identical
    Snowflakes"
The Literary Review: "The Banality of Metaphor"
The Massachusetts Review: "Bony Mares"
The Montserrat Review: "The Wedding at Cana"
Natural Bridge: "Peasants Playing Bowls Outside
    A Village Inn"
New Orleans Review: "The City's Oldest Known Survivor
    of the Great War," "Diagnosis," "Exhibition of a
    Rhinoceros at Venice," and "Rachel's Hair"
Northwest Review: "Minotaur"
Notre Dame Review: "Lot's Wife," "The Physicist,"
    and "Woman Gardening"
Oasis: "Scorpion's Tail"
Passages North: "Breaking Down the Big Top"

The Paterson Literary Review: "The Sick Child"
Poems & Plays: "Gandhi and Tolstoy Correspond"
Poet Lore: "The Library" and "The Parasol"
Poetry International: "The Dead Love Everything"
        and "Enlightenment"
Prairie Schooner: "In Morocco"
Rhino: "Poem Wrapped In Grease Skin"
River Styx: "Luxembourg Gardens At Twilight"
        and "Office of the Dead"
Roanoke Review: "Small Seascape"
The South Carolina Review: "Wine Tasting"
South Dakota Review: "Central Park, 1901"
Sycamore Review: "The Pallbearer"
West Branch: "The Mediterranean"
Xavier Review: "It Was Sunday and I Had Nothing"
Terminus "I Have to Bend Under the Yellow
        Police Tapes"

I'd like, above all, to thank my wife, Sharon, for the great
richness in my life. I am very grateful to Tom Hunley and
Steel Toe Books for believing enough in my work to present
it to a wider audience. My thanks to Alyce and Stan Paddock
for their continuing support over the years. And a special
thanks to Leanne and Rob Porzycki both for the computer
and for all their technological help on this book.

To my wife, Sharon

PEASANTS PLAYING BOWLS
OUTSIDE A VILLAGE INN

The white-shirted bowler is the best.
The serving maid keeps rushing to him,

her hands piled high with mead and rings
of straw she twined herself. The summer

evening is so warm the plows, left
for dead in the fields till morning, turn

over in their shallow graves. A slant rain
that seemed to step out of the forest

drives the players back inside the inn
where wives are held at bay by dinner

and children climb the bright shutters
like moths. It is 1345 and everyone is up

to date. An entertainer juggles rats,
the serving maid grows sleeker by the hour.

The village priest sees the horns of Satan
in the smoke and collapses into the fireplace

from too much prayer and barley. Outside,
just past the trees, the newest kind of death

is whistling to itself and peeling an apple
as if it had all the time in the world.

DIAGNOSIS

There was no sea for her beyond
this version of it. The circle
of sandpipers and small creatures
washed up by the obliging
waves had perfected itself.
The horizon kept backing away
from the day's end and the stranded
western sun turned insomniac,
so she decided to settle right here, right
now, on this rim of sand that seemed so
certain about everything. She would
cobble the various stones and gullies
into a campfire, hammer its smoke
and haze into a livable shack, cook
the wind patterns for her suppers.
So many dead shore things to choose
from for the decorations. She could fall
in love with being skin and water,
scatter her leftover bones as picturesque
as driftwood. So much the better
if her bones were imprinted
with the tiny salt forms
that had gone so wrong inside her.
The walls of caves had fossils embedded in them.
Hieroglyphics in the long corridors
underneath the desert never grew tired
of repeating the name of carver or patron.

LUXEMBOURG GARDENS AT TWILIGHT

If I lived in the nineteenth century
I would take up one of those six-foot long

tapers and go through these gardens
like a butler, touching the tip of flame

to the air itself, leaving in my wake
chandeliers of haze to inform the early evening

and keep night from the marble vases,
the fountain, the concentric flowers, for I know

nothing of this will remain in the morning
when the sun's undiscriminating glare

prowls these lanes like a bully,
cuffing everything into shadow and chalk,

a black and white world where these Victorian
couples, arm in arm, as muted as crinoline,

could no longer stroll, their lives flickering
like fireflies in and out of the manicured paths.

RACHEL'S HAIR

My Great-Aunt Rachel saved her hair.
When I came of age in her eyes,
she took me down into her basement
past a pavilion of cats, throw rugs,
knitted mottoes, and her wedding dress
from 1910 growing ethereal on its rack,
moving slightly as we stirred the air,
as if it were hungry to gobble up
any small yellow light it could
from the basement's one bulb, lit
only on the rarest of occasions. Over
in the corner was a sea chest, though
the only sea changes in the last twenty
years of Aunt Rachel's life were this death
and that, each person coming to attention
by proper name before Aunt Rachel for a brief
inspection between the announcement of the death
and the funeral. When she opened the cedar
lid of the chest, I saw hair packed
two or more feet deep, by individual strand,
by color and anniversary and decade, almost
by century. Aunt Rachel was so pleased
and secretive as she showed it,
I had a sudden fear that perhaps
she was planning to leave it to me
in her will. I touched a few
of the top strands hesitatingly. I knew
at that moment if I pushed my hand
farther down, my hand would disappear
from this side of a lifetime, this moment,
and emerge in the first decade
of the twentieth century, my fingers

heavy with rings and their showcase
faces: cameos in ivory, Tiffany
glass cut into miniature Egyptian
screens, ruby bands, a raw diamond
so fresh from the mines the new
century had yet to walk its hall
of mirrors, its facets, holding Rachel's hand.

I FOUND TWO IDENTICAL SNOWFLAKES

and the whole superstructure
of distinction collapsed. Now my fingerprints
were no longer unique
and I could commit crimes at will.

My DNA sloshed back and forth
in a common stew. Across the universe
there were billions of suns
just like ours.

I published two volumes
on the two snowflakes and a critic
wrote they were also identical
in a thousand ways

I had missed. One leaf
was exactly another, one muscle
always its twin, each child
the first child.

"God doesn't play dice
with the universe," said Einstein
as he came home
in the middle of winter for some

chicken soup, took off his overcoat,
brushed the snow from his hair
and found a third identical flake.
"See," he said.

HANDS AT SEVENTY

The mirror bends over to examine
the tan marks drifting back and forth
across my hands. My skin has drawn

the loose gloves of age over itself.
These hands have melted and re-hardened
too many times, like the unthreaded fiber

in a desert plant. The mirror can see
down to bone, I can see through it.
My fingertips tell me every day that

these are the hands I want right now.
The years when the veins were hidden
behind flesh went by without ever knowing

the time of day. Now I keep a loving
eye on time itself, stroke it intimately
with these hands, to slacken its saw-toothed

traps or coax it into the light to eat
from my fingers. When I decide to stop
feeding time the small scraps it can't do

without, it is these hands that will bequeath
me to the earth. The fingers will grow longer
and thinner as if the only unbreakable habit
were a compulsion to point the way.

EXHIBITION OF A RHINOCEROS AT VENICE

It is 1741, the first time a living
rhinoceros is brought to Europe.

The rhinoceros is led around the courtyard
at the palace of the Doge. A masquerade

ball is taking place. The rhinoceros, who
began history as a unicorn but couldn't

stop taking on armor, blinks at the masks
that approach him and recede in waves.

Some are of wild beasts, some of ancient
spirits. In the corners of his eyes,

glints of light come and go. He cannot
know they are jewels on the hands that brush

his hide quickly and withdraw. The candles
cast his dark armor in twisting shapes

that could be from the jungle. The costumes
of the revellers move in and out of view.

Hoods draw the ivory faces tighter
and tighter. The faces can't stop flickering

as if hesitant light were their mime and chant.
They dance in a circle. The rhinoceros

is at the center, the dark sheen of the past.
The evening is a great success. The Doge

raises a toast to the company, kisses
the hand of his mistress. His servants

wind through the candelabra and guests,
prod the rhinoceros into his burnished cage.

GANDHI AND TOLSTOY CORRESPOND

Note: The Gandhi-Tolstoy letters, which were written in 1909 and 1910, focused on the need for non-violence as an active force, reflecting inner peace and love.

Count Tolstoy brushed the most brutal
Russian winter in over a decade
from his greatcoat as if he were shaking off
after-dinner crumbs and went back
into the house. In South Africa
Mahatma Gandhi woke at 2:00 a.m.
and walked twenty-one miles
to his office in Johannesburg
through a warm fog that scoured
and crystallized distance
so it could be broken at will.

They picked up their pens.

They wrote to each other of something
so far inside the monastery
of the cell it would take all
the technology of the twentieth century
to find it. The Russian Revolution
would come and go, the British
Empire would fall, the atom
would be split before
people could stare down the corridors
of their own bones
and imagine caves, imagine
cathedrals.

They put down their pens.
They looked around and saw death everywhere.
Only the two of them laughed at the joke.

THE CATACOMBS IN ROME

The tourists are allowed
to sample death,
but with stringent restrictions.

The authorities are afraid
priceless artifacts
like the dust from a bone

might leave the catacombs
on a fingertip, might touch
something worldly

and the skeletons
will waver in their meditations,
will sense

it is not God the vaults
are trying to capture,
not the passage of time

which never bothers
the dead, but the still whorls
of a fingerprint

that might be hiding blood,
an airtight box of skin
touch might open again.

WOMAN GARDENING

I want nothing new. I want only
all the words that have been said
before: *sun, trowel, fingernails,*
stem, buskin, water, seed.

The web dirt thins out in a great
arc from the shovel. Inches
below the surface, the earth
makes a fist against steel.

These are the perennials. Words
like root a billion times
turned over and over again
all the years out of the cave.

She unravels the wire cages
into frames, lines straight
enough for crops, up and down
cadence so soil can memorize.

The pitch and furrow of a rake.
A hundred years to find the right
leaf. The slant grain of the proper
hat for first planting. Hands

for a word that floats just above,
floats misshapen like a breakdown
in the bud just before it flowers.
Eyes, lips, runnels, trellises, rain.

POEM WRAPPED IN GREASE SKIN

"You can't take too much care,"
my mother said. Her pores
had evolved into an advanced form
of communication. One biology class
I left the bones of a frog
I had dissected for homework
simmering in the family's soup pot
on our stove. My mother served them
and said, "Let that be a lesson
for us all." So now I soak
edibles in absorbent tissue
and tell people I'm watching
my weight when I'm really
collecting grease to seal
the tar paper cracks in my skin
against wind and snow. There is
no saying for this yet
so I've borrowed from the church:
"Don't try to mop up the dead
with your surplice," the priest
told me when my flowing
altar boy vest got caught
in the rusty hinges
of a cheap casket
at a graveside ceremony
when all the relatives
were circling the grave
in a shuffle and chanting
longer and longer Latin vowels
against the threatening clouds overhead.

14

SCORPION'S TAIL

No use turning over rocks.
The poison comes of its own accord,

crawling like a baby.
And, don't worry, it won't kill,

at least not usually.
If it mistakes your hiking boot

for the desert,
it is a tribute to the elemental pores

through which things emerge.
Heat, darkness, cilia

to prod time along.
There will be no rash spreading

across you
that I can't rub into something else

for both of us.
Think of the elaborate architecture

of the tail,
the microscopic girders, the secret

compartments, mortar, the aisles
for one-celled acolytes

to construct their altars.
It would be an honor

to live at such a level
for that instant.

THE SICK CHILD

They bribed her with bright
stories and visions of angels.
They brought a game with spinning
wheels the colors of jam —
boysenberry, apricot, chokecherry.

They needed her on her side
facing them so they could
monitor her, so the brown,
three-dimensional air could drain
more easily from her lungs.

She turned for them or maybe
just to stare at the door
between them. I imagined her
willing the door closer
and closer to herself, but she could

just as easily have been holding
it at bay. Her parents
spent hours on their knees
praying. I brought water
with cracked ice. I was a volunteer

on a hospital ward of toys
and bald heads. The children
were always more grateful to me
than they should have been
for their age. I am selfish, want

a clear ending to her story — death
or remission for a lifetime —
but the girl was transferred
from the hospital, beyond the reach
of anyone except those with a claim —

doctors and family. That was
the summer before I went to college
forty years ago. The faces
from then have no features
anymore. The small bodies move

like ritual blurs behind a screen
of gauze. But my hands still feel
the powdery moss of the latex gloves
we had to wear against all soiled things:
cups, bedsheets, pajamas, rocking horses.

GOING FROM THE PAINTINGS
TO THE DESERT

1
The stone bends over
as if it has become too delicate
for its own weight,
as if it is looking down
for a harpsichord
or some other transparent instrument
to play. It is one of the great
stone flowers
painted over and over
by Georgia
O'Keeffe, the place settings
of polished bone
on desert flatland.

2
Though there is nothing
intangible in this New Mexican
landscape, everything
I reach for
recedes from my fingertips.
Touch has to imagine
me, as if I were
the gallery, and the museum
pieces were constantly
on my right or left,
too far beyond
to doubt
any possibility.

3

I am incidental
to the dry air which holds
the sky and rock in place. If the air
were ever to shift,
even an inch, the entire desert
would crack
like porcelain into shards
I could rub
between my fingers.
But, though my fingers wore away,
I could never polish the shards
back to the sheen
around me today
when the reflections,
like the water that isn't here,
seem to erode me,
and I begin
to imagine myself the rock
that is no longer here.

LOT'S WIFE

Joy was as easy as bitterness, so she turned
to choose the pillar of salt that framed

all directions at once and seasoned the bland
air with possibilities neither the cities behind

nor the God above remembered for her. Who wouldn't
want fire rather than burial wax fixed

in the eyes forever? When Lot took their daughters
by the hands and refused to look back at her,

she realized how glad she was to be free
of the wandering. God was one promise after another,

dragging her family towards Zoar, towards the mountains,
towards a wavering future made in God's own

restlessness. And the cities she left behind drifted
back and forth with the sand in their streets.

So she imagined herself crystal to strip the wind
of its future and gloss the aimless desert with a center

and she turned.

THE LIST

The day looks overgrown with common
household burrs. So does the dog. The kettle
sits up at the thought of boiling grease. This
is a measure I can take against complacency.

The list, I mean. The essential things to do
written down both arms, calling for action
before they harden into the past, like scabs,
or into the irreplaceable future, like tattoos.

Too late. I have grown up and have taken
to reading the words backwards in the mirror.
I've married, though that wasn't on the list.
My wife says I still have the same old ambitions.

Day by day. Liver spots blotting the most
important words, soiling my carefully made
deathbed. The dog warty, the kettle whistling,
creeper vines from the burrs growing over me.

EXILE IN JAPAN

He washes his hands in the stream
and dries them on the cherry blossoms.

The water of his home province will run
through his wife's fingers when she lifts

them to her lips. His children are still
asleep though they have kicked the quilt

to the floor. The farmers here wear
the same bamboo hats and walk beside

the same oxen. The soil churns up
as slowly as the foam in the coast's

shallows. Those pools are up to his knees
and the tides of an ocean between him and China.

The day is at his waist now and rising
more quickly. Soon it will be over his head,

his only thought to keep from drowning.
So many thoughts he has already mistaken for breath.

THE CITY'S OLDEST KNOWN SURVIVOR
OF THE GREAT WAR

marches in uniform down the traffic stripe
at the center of the street, counts time
to the unseen web that has rearranged
the air around him, his left hand
stiff as a leather strap along his side,
the other saluting right through the decades
as if they weren't there, as if everyone under ninety
were pervasive fog the morning would dispel
in its own good time, as if the high school band
all flapping thighs and cuffs behind him
were as ghostly as the tumbleweed on every road
dead-ended in the present, all the ancient infantry
shoulder right, through a skein of bone, presenting arms
across the drift, nothing but empty graves now
to round off another century,
the sweet honey of the old cadence, the streets
going by at attention, the banners glistening with dew,
the wives and children blowing kisses.

CENTRAL PARK, 1901

The buildings aren't tall enough
yet to contain the park. It casts
a trawling net of leaves
and late sun across the city streets,

draws in a catch of ladies
and amber parasols and gentlemen
strolling together with the whole
century before them for the taking.

The pale green benches that ring
the park like an Elizabethan collar
fill up before the dinner hour
with twelve-year-old girls

in stockings of white lace.
The girls are wearing on either side
parents who, rumor has it,
were brought across the Atlantic

by special courier in shipments
usually reserved for Florentine marble.
The parents' sole purpose is to set off
the daughters. The sleek carriages

and the horses drawing them
seem to billow rather than move
up and down along the park's
lanes in lines that are never

more than a centimeter off. One
woman tells her husband
that the carriages are black sails
and the horses are mahogany

carvings for the prows. The woman
is wearing a whalebone corset
that leaves nothing for a waist
but a silk ruffle and a wedding

ring. Her husband lifts his top hat
to her. As if that were a signal,
the sun drops behind the trees
and the couple leaves for dinner.

The park begins to empty. Angles
that went unnoticed before
sharpen now as if twilight
were a whetstone for honing

trees and bushes. It is too late.
It is night. The park is moving,
a huge dark vessel, slowly
through the years toward us.

MINOTAUR

The fools have given me a monastery,
a vestal order, shadows in procession

along every wall, slim novitiates of love.
They value their Mediterranean virgins

as I value the twists of thought down stone
corridors. Everyone entering this labyrinth

takes a vow of silence. The labor of solving
damp walls and all the skins shed

against the tightening rock trim back
the darkness until answers are everywhere.

And then these fools. Dull Theseus. Ariadne
trailing her ledger of strings, tallying

answers which cancel each other out.
In the sunlight, so little matters

that yes and no seem profound. I roam
miles of nerve endings, coiled, bloodless,

striking at random. My horns impale
whatever hesitates between gods.

DESERT MOTEL

It was a place where time
had edges, where the face
of the clock was sand.

The segmented wooden units
adhered loosely, like cracks,
like irregular squares

marked out on the shell
of some insect working its
way through the hours.

The town of two hundred
was ten miles away. There
was nothing for another

hundred miles in any
direction. I lived there
for a month, to discard

some dried-out and excess
time like a dead skin
from my life. I wanted

to remove all distractions
from the sun so it
could do the work

it was born for: peeling
away paint, clothing,
shrubs, pavement, flesh.

I left when my pores
were raw enough for new
coverings, new breaths,

for air that didn't stay
in the same parched place,
marking it like a monument,

but came and went at will,
for a rabble of incursions
bent on storming the brain.

THE ELEPHANT BURIAL GROUND

Walking in processional
on either side of the elephants
are their attendant nurses:
gazelles no longer addicted
to speed, zebras wrinkling
black and white by turns, giraffes
to search out like periscopes
ambushes lying in wait ahead.

It takes days, months, years.
The trail is often muddy. They watch
for broken bottles, unusual colors,
smoldering tires on the path.
In each village they go through
the sidewalks are lined with people
who have removed their hats and tongues.
The bedridden watch from windows.

More and more decide to join them.
Lions look up from the soft
underbelly of their kill and decide
they have had enough. Parrots
ride the elephants' backs like bright
coachmen, splashes of green and yellow
against the tough grey. It is becoming
harder and harder to believe in death.

There are humans, too, though you
have to look hard among all
that size and number. If the parade
gets any larger, there will be
no more secrets. Everyone will know
where the elephant burial ground
is. There will be mounds so high
hordes will live forever in the shade.

THE MEDITERRANEAN

"Eye, canvas, sapphire, mirror, lantern."
It's all been said, he thought, as he stripped

the spinnaker to catch the flex and blade
of a soft aluminum wind. The Mediterranean

backpedalled in the wake of his sailboat, the water
skimming itself in parallel lines. He opened

his hand for the air's ravenous atoms. The sun
held nothing back. He was too far from the sight

of shore for the usual categories. The indivisible water
was as breathable as the sky. He bowed slightly

from the waist and it seemed to him the Mediterranean
bowed back. It took the boat from him. The current

was a series of intricate moves as small and stylized
as an eighteenth-century minuet. The surface of the water

held itself still, a formal blue to match
the elegance of the atoms he held in his palm

and the various designs turning their corners
as they tumbled in slow motion through his veins.

OFFICE OF THE DEAD

He carried her body into the cemetery
in his arms. He would bury her

himself. They were married sixty years.
No children. Relatives and friends dead.

She was almost pure bone. The little
flesh she had at the end was so sheer

he thought of it as her last negligee,
as white as the one she wore that night

over half a century ago. It was night, now.
The ground was soft after the rain.

Her body would no longer bruise. He laid
her down on the wet earth. The wind

blew a few leaves against her side.
He got the shovel from the truck and began.

This is the way they would be together
from now on. He had hours to dawn

and tomorrow's caretaker. The shovel seemed
lighter all the time. Surely the ground

worked with him. This was the chore
neither he nor the ground could ever relinquish.

He asked her to be patient. There were so many
things worth waiting for. Veins no longer

on the surface, birthdays outrunning every
tremor but the earth's. His recitative

was the quilt they curled up inside.
She had always kissed with her eyes closed.

THE PHYSICIST

He sits at his desk, a mime pretending
nothing itself is solid. Around him, walls
have thickened, multiplied to the ends
of the continent. He is the only motion.

He is the only stasis, the necessary pivot
at the center. Matter is a streaming dance
the observer is too dense to see
without sliding his fit of equations

over its sexy contours for a sleek,
redundant leotard. He edges himself
aside. The atoms are packed so tightly
against each other, he can't see

between them. But he can see through them.
The empty space inside each atom
is vaster than a desert, so his eye
has nowhere to go but on and on.

He can see through the walls surrounding
his desk, his house, his children
playing in the yard. When he mimics
reaching for a handful of sand,
the universe shrinks from his touch.

IN THE PASTURE

Cows to my left, dead deer to my right.
Cud you could skim rocks over, as taut
as the skin of sea water before it breaks
out into storm waves. Over two million
six hundred thousand blades of grass where
algae would be if this were ocean floor. How
do I know it's not? That white haired guy
over there with maple syrup running down
from the corners of his eyes is Robert Frost.

Around the bend is the valley where Wordsworth
has sat with his legs crossed for the last
two hundred years. Nothing will grow on that
spot, so he is writing poems about vistas.
There's the mountain he has never been up.
Sunsets even the illiterate can enjoy. Look at
that one, pulling a plow with his shoulders,
nude from the waist down, trailing behind
him a line of critics arguing confused symbolism.

If this weren't a pastoral, I wouldn't have
to introduce you to a shepherd. But there
he is, doing something I hope is consensual
with his sheep. I'm glad my mother
didn't come out for this stroll with me.
I'd have to tip the deer onto their noses
so she'd think they were grazing. She
adores Nature. The last time I walked her
through it, I made sure she was blindfolded.

BREAKING DOWN THE BIG TOP

When the circus is ready to discard a town
as swiftly as a movie star
with an endless line
of waiting lovers
discards the latest one,
I am the agent of departure,

the supervisor
who gestures with his hand
and a row of elephants walks off
with the center poles
like spangled plows
churning the dust behind them.

The tent floats down
swallowing the air as it goes
and breaking out into waves along the ground.
When you look up
the sky is itself once more
as if a canvas robe had slipped from its shoulders.

The lines of rigging
are the collapsible horizons
we carry with us to the next town.
The lights rise from them
to cue the overtures.
What we leave behind are encores.

I conduct the day
to its vanishing point. Where ton
after ton folds into its own corners
as tightly as a handkerchief. Where trucks
rise like shoals out of the dusk
and capsize into the night.

IN THE WINE COUNTRY OF SPAIN

The juice of the sun and grapes
runs down my arms, which fray red
and purple by turns. I hope the stains
are indelible. Here the vines
grow out of pores in the earth. This
is where I want to be buried. The country
of urns and vases, and of the shoulders
of the great bulls turning in their sleep
under the soil, where our flesh will run
into each other's. Beneath my bare
feet, the earth reluctantly turns
to the draw of the sun and its string
of planets. Because the earth here
is always on the verge of stopping,
the soil has grown dark and thick.
The vineyards take what they want
from the sun and give the rest back.
If I could hold a vineyard
in the palm of my hand, the dead
would never know thirst again.
When I lie down on the ground,
I can hear the sad tumult of water
so far below the surface that I believe
the water is in me, and its impossible weight
will keep me from ever rising again.

BONY MARES

Two for a shilling. Fare
thee well. The trees
shingled to the low
clouds. The furrows

tough as lines
of oak, bouncing every plow
back. The mares
worn clean through,

their overlapping skins tenuous
as fog. No seeds
that won't turn black,
shunting marble

jags to crack the soil.
The English farmer
blesses the new year,
1784, and grinds

the air into flakes
for the mares to digest.
The brook weeps
through his house

and his family wears
woolen underwear to scratch
themselves clean. Bony
mares and another shilling

left over for drink. The children
ride the mares in place.
His wife blushes
with brambles. English

soil is the best soil
in the world
for burying. Everything goes
away. Everything keeps.

IN MOROCCO

Around the corner, the edge of the desert
dissolves into pebbles as it washes up

against the antique troughs. The light
ties itself into a sailor's knot at eye

level and won't budge until evening,
so everyone has to walk around it

right into the center of the Sahara.
There are rumors that the brusque

scarves on the faces only unravel
for death or sex. Everything else

is an illusion that buzzes around us
in its tiny cocoons. The spider across

my wall gets caught in its own web
and has to eat its way out. As its bites

become slower and slower, the room
turns on its axis for the landlord

sun at both ends of the day. Light
left over from the year before

turns the sand green, into crystal glass,
for minutes at a time but nothing ever breaks.

THE PALLBEARER

I carry the coffin because I came across it
at the beginning of my walk this evening.

Three corners were already taken, so I hoisted
the remaining one onto my shoulder and continued

walking. For all I know the body inside
is a stranger's. Though you can get acquainted

with a person by the weight and this one
is so light the four of us pallbearers

could walk tightwires to the cemetery.
I might sway a bit just to tease

the crowd of mourners following our moves
from the bleacher seats eighty feet below.

Perhaps the coffin is made out of balsa wood,
or perhaps the bones inside went to balsa wood

just before death. I have been told disease
or prayer equally will lighten you, though

I might end up having to depend on disease
since my mother fed herself a steady diet

of irreverence when she was pregnant with me.
Maybe something with wings imprinted itself

at the birth of the person inside the coffin
and an inclination to religion followed naturally.

Well, here we are at the grave. Time to lower
the coffin, say a few words for the deceased,

and be on my way. Such a beautiful evening.
The best part of the day for meeting people.

CRACKED LIPS

The air is tight. There are seams in her lips,
no seams in the air. No reason to talk

that is not painful. Each time she runs
her tongue over the cracks they feel wider.

Soon the blood will start. She wants him
to kiss her now, but he goes on talking.

They each gesture with separate tickets.
I have to imagine everything anyway so

I assign different busses. The station is packed
with people, baggage, tickets. It is impossible

but there is a bus for everyone. If
the listed destination is not the one you want,

write yours in large block letters
and paste it over the printed one in the glass

rectangle above the front window of the bus.
The driver will then have no choice

but to take you there. I am okay, though.
My bus is on schedule. The air is loosening.

The blood on her lips is starting in tiny
drops. There is no cause for concern yet,

but I hope she won't try to speak.
I hope I'll be gone before she does.

THE WEDDING AT CANA

The black marrow in the eyes of Christ
drained the room. No separate life remained,
not the drunken guests twisting back and forth
in their chairs as if they couldn't breathe, not
the bride and groom who had receded
into the silver nitrate of old photographs, not
his own mother swathed in the shroud
that disfigures love and flesh.
                                    Water
is a scythe. It can cut a furrow
a mile deep through a million years
of mountain. It can strip
the topsoil from the farmland
in an afternoon. The great stone jars
were lined up before him in a phalanx. He walked
their rows as if admiring a reservoir
of power contained and bottled
for the future. Then he turned his back
abruptly and left the feast. A fine amber
film started to form across the liquid.

THE DEAD LOVE EVERYTHING

Earth or river. Wind or flame.
It all slides through their bony
fingers. Nothing weighs
too slight or too heavy, a feather
against the world they wanted
so passionately to join. Eyes
that grew bigger and bigger
until only the skull
could hold them. Ears
disappearing at the highest
pitch, smell tracking
every path the same. They reached
out, farther and farther, until touch
came undone, detached
itself, and we can feel
it here, in the grasses, or there,
in the way fog grows heavier
and descends over us, a grey shift
to wear through the morning. Theirs
are the voices that come through suddenly
with the right metaphor, the right sound
drummed out by the relentless lungs
in place of air.

THE TOWER OF BABEL

For years they had been investing
sun-dried bricks in an account
that would buy them heaven.

It was time to live on the principal.
Houses of clay raced each other
across the Plain of Shinar, suburbs

around a transparent castle, around
the idea of a castle, cascading levels
that would rise and rise above themselves

back to a beginning in the sky.
Workers streamed by the thousands
into the houses. It would take

a hundred years of sons and daughters
to break free from the block-and-tackle
of blood holding them like a tow line

to the earth. The ascent to God
began with kilns and burnt fingers
and red mud so deep under the pores

it would seed their bones in the grave.
It was only later when they mistook
language for divinity that they realized

death was a word they held in the palms
of their hands, the same in every country,
one that would disappear if you blew upon it.

THE BLUE DRESS

My Great-Aunt Rachel dipped
her fingers into the folds
of the nineteenth century and drew out
a great swath of that sky
layered with nothing but itself
for the last time.
Her skin was always cream and modish.
The blue cloth surged
against the thimbles on her fingertips,
against her grey will,
into the gown she would wear
ever after, like the ending
of a fairy tale or a parable, to celebrate
biblical times: marriages,
births, funerals. She died before
I was a teenager.
Everything about her is a grainy photograph
except the gown.
I asked her once, after overhearing
my parents, if she wanted
to be buried in that dress. She seemed
to draw its pleats around her
like a fan. I didn't recognize
flirtation at the time
but now I imagine her eyes softening,
measuring death
for a gentleman worthy of her.
She shook her head no.
When she turned away, all the bustle
of the dress brushed her body
like a watercolor, and I realized for the first time
the sway of pastel underneath.

VITAMINS

If there are others out there
who also take twenty-three
pills at a time four times
every day, please contact me
through the personals. We can
help each other force them down.
I will say they are tiny sandbags
keeping things on course. You'll reply
they are the flow itself, the *Tao*.
We will look shyly at each other.
We will start to kiss. Together
we will feel them ooze and sidle
in teams through the digestive
tract like synchronized swimmers.
Who else will know your insides
like me? The warm flush of waves
when that orange horse pill hits
the blood like a boulder. The fizz
of cartilage holding itself together
for another six hours. Time release
capsules for dry bones, bleached
desert rats gulping down canteen
after canteen. What couple could
have more in common than a continual
dissolving? I am a young seventy-nine.
Looking for a minimum taker of sixty
pills daily. Call me if you want
to twist some tops off. Let's rattle
the bottles till they're gone. Smokers okay.

SMALL SEASCAPE

I have my head so close
to a tidal pool in the rocks
I could be fishing with my nose,
trying to replace air with water
as my face's natural limit
and magnifying glass. What I see
are grits with no eyes
and barely enough body, swimming,
darting, cutting right angles
and a sudden hypotenuse
into an element that can't hold
for more than a turn or two
the quart of water the last wave
could spare by a factor
in the millions. If a crab
were my centerpiece in this instant
living room, liquid, porous,
ready to collapse itself
and travel to the next site
at a moment's notice
like a miniature circus,
I'd be so taken by size
and recognizable shape, I'd miss
the real performers, the fleas,
the specks, incidental networks
of perpetual motion, turning
their tricks like pros
no matter how movable the hoops,

the stages, they are given,
no matter how gargantuan
their competitors, how capricious
the ocean they seem
to have no trouble
reducing to size.

ON THE WIDOW'S WALK

She trims her aprons to the Atlantic wind
as her husband must be trimming the sails
of the four-master he shipped out on, overdue

for ten months now. She starts and ends
every day on this wooden platform, wobbly
at the rock's edge, leaning to the sand below

like a dowsing rod that can find water
by the oceanful but not one human body.
Over the years she has learned

the art of looking between the salt flecks
in the air's spray. She can see
nothing farther and farther out each time.

But she has children to raise
two miles back in the house he built
for her. A slathering together of planks,

a poor job to the farmers around here,
their feet hewn from the soil
like tree stumps. But decent enough

for a man like her husband, whose legs
swayed and gave only on solid land
as if it ran porous with currents

he could never see coming. He built
precision ships in the bottles
he finished off while waiting for his next berth

until she had a fleet under glass
for bartering in town
when he was away at sea

and the pay ran out. She can tell now
by the rising sting the usual storm
is blowing in from the east so she turns

to go with her daily promise
never to give up coming to this bare tower
even if her husband returns home.

NO INTRODUCTIONS NECESSARY

I lay pennies on the track
and wait for a train to come.

The pennies only get older.
A tramp announces the great age

of railroads is over. The boxcars
have settled down in suburbia

and constructed white picket fences
around themselves. I leave the pennies

there anyway. They can play at being
ghost coins for a runaway locomotive

from the past. I would love to stand
in its path and let it pass through me.

Do you hear the dead laughing? No one
can take the past away from them.

That's why they feel so secure in the earth,
why I, their future, can walk and walk

and never walk away. Admit it. You're
more like me than you thought. Flesh

is the most transparent illusion. Take the coins
before they're distorted and put them on your eyes.

WINE TASTING

It is too old and expensive
to spit out. I curry it
under my tongue. The lighting
is soft, romantic for rack
after rack of cobwebbed bottles.

Soon the aftertaste will swell
and take me back a century
to the vines. I'll break grapes
in halves, then fourths, eighths,
smear my arms to the elbows.

I'll speak French and swing
great loaves of bread along afternoon
strolls over the curves of Provence.
I'll catch salt on my fingertips.
Vineyards will eat out of my hands.

"This wine will go well with cheese,"
I say as stupidly as possible. When
they turn away, I tilt the bottle
and the last hundred years slides
down my throat as easily as breathing.

IT WAS SUNDAY AND I HAD NOTHING

to do so I went to church.
According to the preacher, according

to John, Christ was the first
begotten of the dead. The second,

third, and fourth were sitting
in front of me. I looked around,

clearly superior to the gods
and their worshippers from the Roman

Empire on, and ducked. The stained
glass was skimming little slates

of blood across the congregation, beheading
its tallest members. A statue

of Mary screamed in labor. The ceiling,
a gigantic cross, started to collapse. Everyone

had turned towards me. Some were
holding their babies up. The huge

doors seemed a thousand miles away.
I don't know how I clawed my way out

but I stood on the street, dripping
with their smiles, with the laughter I still

heard. There were stains on my clothes
that I haven't identified to this day.

THE LIBRARY

All around me, books were dissolving.
Waterfalls of dust poured from the shelves.

It started with the one I was reading.
As I turned a page, the print faded,

the paper grew backward into brown
parchment, the binding started to flow.

I looked around. One book after another
was growing fainter and fainter, then going

out, like the moment when dusk is finally
quenched or when a drop of juice turns

dry and sour in the corner of your mouth.
I found myself waist-deep in a pile of silt.

Clouds of powder wheeled around me, ghosts
beating their grey wings against the ceiling.

THE BANALITY OF METAPHOR

"No, no, not night but death"
— W.B. Yeats

I imagine ways to die.
The hunter lays his stone axe
at the center of a circle of ashes.
It is what has always been done.
The blood running out of him
changes color as it touches the floor
of the cave. It becomes indistinguishable
from the dirt. Across the rock walls
are the animals he has painted.
He shuts his eyes, stunned
that his life is as slight as theirs.

I had to close my father's eyes
because he died staring. What
I saw before me at that instant
was as insignificant and anonymous
a collection of molecules
as the caveman a million years
after his death. Everything
that would be was, no matter
how many rites my family
and I had yet to go through.
My father was an honest person.
In his last seconds, he looked
straight at me with shock
and then pity, as if he had just
realized his son's life was
as slight as his, as everyone's.

THE FERRIS WHEEL

He kicks the lights at his feet
into a fairway, a field, a town,
dice rolling everywhere
beneath him, fireflies with dark
eyes hitting seven, eleven
on the first turn. He stretches

his arms across the back
of the seat and puffs his mouth
into gargoyle cheeks. He rises
over the cathedral's highest
curve like a heathen with wings.
The moon comes at him

and he flails it down. Above
the clouds now, night
on its side, the cold air
through his arms, the whirr
and gear of the crankcase
whistling spangles into skin.

Ride after ride until the farmland
greys and he realizes
it is the earth turning
again, another day on solid
ground, up to his knees
in scattered fog.

The bulbs at the center
of his palms wink
back and forth. Time
to close his fists,
wring out the bright baubles,
let them into his blood.

EVE WITH BERRY NECKLACE

It was the first time
Adam saw her undressed.

She got the idea from leaves,
moss climbing

out of the sun's rich stain.
God's narrowed

eyes behind her, and Adam blind
for the first time.

Touch was the name they gave it.
The future started

down the tree with a different name,
knowledge,

which the Bible would settle on sooner
or later.

God dissolving into the exclusion
of the serpent

and the garden around them
beginning

its slow wheel into the seasons,
the newest

thing of all, disappearing life,
budding.

THE SERENGETI,

stained in green, paws
the sky, and the wind
answers, sorts the grass
into proper rivulets.

Cheetahs roll in sand,
an unlikely tic
for one of the fastest
animals across a scree,

the mountain petulant
against the rain.
The lions are eyeing
the weakest elephant

and dreaming sit-down
family dinners for a week.
The cubs are over-achieving
with a late antelope.

I palm the Serengeti
with the newest camera,
but when I open my hand
later in New York

nothing is there
but faint reflections
of ivory sliding
softly along my lifelines,

maybe sunspots, maybe
hidden burial grounds,
maybe a string of marshes
carved into a necklace.

BROTHER AND SISTER IN COMAS

On a double bed, cranked forward
so liquids won't collect to swell
the brains, they drift like dry
leaves against the invisible window

hospital workers watch them through.
Volunteers read to them in shifts,
hoping their pores mistake the words
for air and suck them in. Maybe

stray language can dollop firmness
in microscopic shards to the cells,
shapeless and free-floating in the bloat
of twenty-four hour IV's. The mother

smoothes the sheet between them as often
as it bunches up, so they can sense
each other without ridges or any other
interruption. The doctors keep instructing

the father in the mechanics of the body,
that memory is a diagram as insular
in its hard edges as the nervous system,
as paralyzed when a cable snaps on itself.

If the bodies must be moved to a hospital
of last resort, nurses skilled in wedging
non-existent time between the seasons
will keep them alive for the infinity

accident insurance allows. The mother
goes on thinning the contours of the space
between them. They are wings on either side
breaking from the cocoon she strokes away.

THE BLACKBERRIES

Like hordes of dusk,
the blackberries threw us
back against the barn walls
that summer, swarmed into
the calving stalls, poured down
from the hayloft in dark
waterfalls, curbed and eddied
in whirlpools around the grain.
We hefted stains and juices
in our palms like piles of coins,
tumbled them through our fingers.
Our violet arms turned dense
to the elbows, our jeans
turned flannel with the husks.
We couldn't wait to grow
second and third skins, night
with its silkiness, cocoons
tight and sticky.

If it rained frogs, locusts,
fireflies that summer, we wouldn't
have noticed. We lounged around
in drenched wheelbarrows
and rusted tubs popping
blackberries to the beat
of hit tunes from the forties.

We pulled socks of blackberry
wine up around our ankles, spit
blue blood like sixteenth-
century kings, flecked our retinas
so royal the slow membrane
of the sky steeped itself
in purple sugar, drew
our eyes heavy and closed
against remorseless suns,
dandelion Junes, our own
weightlessness as baroque
as any season ought to be.

YOUNG FARMERS IN THEIR SATURDAY BEST

On the rock at the ocean's edge,
the gypsy bullfrogs stare
across the waves, wondering
where to start.

Tonight there'll be a new moon,
Saturday village, a roundelay
at the new barn, with any luck
a visiting musician.

Along the roads, the farmers head
towards the big dance. They don't even
wave goodbye to the fields or heighten
new seed beds

one last time. The farmers wash out
from the shore, out where currents
are thick at their arms and legs
with legends of mermaids.

In the stories, the kiss of a princess
is enough for a happy ending. The farmers
sport maple canes from the feed store,
detachable collars.

There is a whirlpool at their feet
as they dance. The wooden boards part
beneath them and they begin to drop
straight down,

one couple after another, swim away
into their true fins. The light that can't
make it to this depth and the pressure that can
glide by their bodies.

EGGSHELLS

We can't open the cupboard
because it is packed
with Aunt Mariah's eggshells.

She has pasted them together
with cocoon glue,
painted them blue and rosy.

The cupboard is part of a larger
art work entitled
Eggshell Apocalypse, but Aunt

Mariah has had creator's block
for years and can't
get past staring at the cupboard

with a live hen in her hands.
As one hen dies,
we replace it with another.

Mom says it is the burden
of having an artist
in the family. The eggshells

are pretty and Aunt Mariah
says her art
has a life-or-death message

for the world. When the world
comes around,
we'll hear the message just like

the one Our Lady of Lourdes
or Fatima gave
those kids which, the nuns said,

is locked up in a Vatican vault
until the end
of the world or perhaps just before it.

Aunt Mariah says anything opened
too soon
is an eggshell and that includes

the world itself, presents, books,
flower boxes,
sex, ancient wonders, and hope.

Maybe even hens, I think
to myself
as she hands me the latest one.

AT THE AUTOMAT

The dog choke-chained to the only blue
hydrant in New York presses one

toothy grin after another against the blue
humid air stalking the sidewalk and alley

of the automat. Inside, the people look out,
the rising level of peanut butter and jelly

sandwiches so glad in their eyes that tears
stick to the retinas. Someone low and oily

with a wine bottle in a paper bag feeds
the dog an old chip. A wobbling grackle

mistakes a parking ticket for a return
map to the wildlife preserve. The rest

of the day rocks back and forth, loitering
or panhandling on the corner. I scratch

my initials in the nickel cake on my plate
to celebrate my twelfth birthday. Truant

again and nobody to catch me in a city
as big as this. I win a staring contest

with the dog, flip the wino off, and toss
my subway token home into a beggar's cup.

THE PARASOL

Every time she went out,
my Great Aunt
Rachel dueled the sun
to a standstill.
The pages of the family
photo album flare
with her parasol. Its oriental
pastels slyly leak
through the black and white
streets, the sepia
backyards, the amber picnics
with horse and carriage
idling in the background against
a grove of elms.
Aunt Rachel believed flesh
was a mistake,
perhaps the slightest slip
of God's hands
as they shaped the sixth day
of Genesis. She
spent her life accordingly,
keeping skin
in the shadows. The drapes
were always drawn
in her house. By the front
door the parasol
stood ready for combat
in its oaken stand
like the sheathed sword
of a knight, his charm

against the next medieval dragon.
When she opened
her parasol outside, it was a carousel
of pink and blue,
the only sky ever allowed
to spin above her.

THOSE WERE THE DAYS, I GUESS

I took a bath every Saturday night for church.
The Missouri trees lined up outside the window
to watch. My mother made me scrub
until I was pink like gum. I watched
each new line on my skin carefully
to see how far it would run
for each new mark of height I put on.

My grandfather owned a harness and wagon
shop in the town. He said that people
were changing. More bought for ornaments
now than use. He died and my grandmother
sealed the shop. None of the things belonged
to anyone until my grandmother died. Then
my father sold the shop and bought our car.

My mother said the pastor at our church
was too old to watch television. He didn't
know what everyone was talking about. My sister
said we were the eleventh family in the town
to get a set. I drew a television screen
in the dirt with a stick so I could see
the ants more clearly. The wind blew it away.

When I was six we moved. My father said
it was time to trade the overalls for a good suit.
I spit six times in the dirt before we left
because I didn't know if you could spit
in the city. I tried to think what to fill
my pockets with. When we drove away, I said
I was a dog running after our car, barking

at the tires, thirsty to bite the next thing
that would hold still. I threw a flat penny
from the railroad tracks out the window
of the car. The trees couldn't go by fast
enough for us. We sang gospel songs
and cheered every time we passed a car.
It was the first time we drove all night long.

MARCO POLO

found the old gods again
in swords and tea leaves,
robes and hanging waves.

Marco Polo crossed himself
before the emperor. He saw
the gold dust the emperor wore

for eyes as the ancient
Romans saw the vinegar
in Christ's side. Marco Polo

wrote a gospel. Every page
changed with every reading
into something three-dimensional

that filled up every blank
in the unexplored world
with a density to flatten

time. Marco Polo held
his book by the binding
and shook the pages out.

Year after year fluttered
down like snow, like birds
from the emperor's cage

so light they never opened
their wings as they rose
and fell on currents of breath.

BREADLINE

The breadline, ninety-six men long,
wears a metal hat so it can count

the rain, wears heirloom sunglasses
so the bread will look toasted,

wears newsprint for glossy shoes
to wade through the optimistic headlines

of the Depression Thirties. The breadline,
nine-hundred-and-forty-three men long,

stands at parade rest, soup ladles shoulder
right to satisfy the next warm vat

of philanthropists. The breadline wriggles
piping hot in the sun to crust over

old radishes. Hands down the row
are garnished with knobs and bristles

so whatever they pick up lingers on.
The eyes are savvy for the impending

juice pumps behind the curtains. Mouths know
how each disappearing trick is performed. The line

is ninety-thousand-and-twelve men long,
so it takes a while, maybe a record,

to pass a bowl down. All those legs
coming unhinged as the line moves forward.

ENLIGHTENMENT

When the drowned man left home
that day, everyone
agreed breathing water was the next

giant step for our species — everyone
being his fellow seekers
in the garden. Only their heads

were visible above the topsoil.
They were performing
the famous flower imitation, seeking

the great crossover when their buried
torsos would intertwine
like roots and they would see petals

whirling in each other's eyes. The drowned
man is a loner.
His head bobs by itself among the seaweed.

The bottom crawlers don't know what
to make of it,
so they start to nibble. He understands

the great pressure the ocean is under.
Maybe he is drowned,
but he is not stupid. Parts of his body

break off and float away in different
directions. His down-current
arm seems to be waving back at him.

He has to laugh. Imagine settling for roots,
when you can go everywhere
at once. His last thought before enlightenment.

JOHN PHILIP SOUSA,

I'd like to invite you to my town,
which has fallen through the cracks
between Kansas and Nebraska, which
is lying back with its hands behind its head
and daydreaming, which is still romantic,
still as skeptical as ever, still waiting
for Main Street to fill up with batons,
for you to wave your arm and part
July's monochromatic heat with an overture
that bends trees right to the pavement
and catapults the lost decades
over the town, the sky gold again
with brass and plumage, the old flags
climbing out of basement windows and streaming
down the streets, the marble drummers
unfurling time from the ancient war monuments,
and the graveyard alive with the woodwinds.

John Philip Sousa, I'd settle for
your bones teaching the earth percussion,
the slow rumble over the horizon
just before a rain, the tuning of the air,
the gathering of colors, the rising arc
of a marching band in the sun's halo
behind the storm clouds as they come over
the hill, the downpour beating time
against the soil and the lightning pinning
its sashes of primary color across the fields.

TOO BAD

Too bad the dinosaurs are dead
but all the dogs
are running back to us
with the bones in their mouths,
fetching them from the steamy plains
where the Jurassic Age had hurled them.

Too bad the Neanderthals are extinct
but all the caves
are drumming out their echoes
and tourist lines are forming
in miners' hats with lights
to walk the burial sites and cull
holy water from the stalactites.

Too bad the Dark Ages are asleep
but all the plagues
are turning in their beds
with night sweats and one eye
open on the luminous clock
for the next dawn with its heaviest
work shift ever and no breaks
for good behavior.

Too bad the millennium is over
but all its romances
are feeding their children
the old calendars, page by page,
so they can overrun the new age
with their appetites and buff the plains
glassy with pearls and bones.

IN CUZCO

The stones are cobbled over the beggar's
ankles as he strikes his way down
the street. The winds are specimen,
a sliced cross-section of the market
that everyone can eat without growing
old. The women's hats have brims
which fit perfectly, whatever the season.

Tomorrow I will cross the river, wait
for the surge in the small railway
to rise to Macchu Picchu. If I'm lucky,
the clouds up there will seep through me
on their way to the next mountaintop.
The high rain will stay in my pores
long enough to lose my way back.

Today in the marketplace, the blankets
are laid out so the crops can grow through
them and be sold whole as they come out
of the earth. The blind beggar points
his cane at me. Surely I can find something
to take back to the hotel. Surely tomorrow
my life will change as I walk away from it.

THE BIRD WATCHER

fiddles for the great finned gull,
almost an albatross, fanning
the thin-skinned tide out
and unraveling the stitches
of the current so no one can sew

it back together. The bird watcher
balances a one-legged flamingo
on his fingertip, knows
as deeply as fire crests that under
the bird's squawking it is pleased

at its unruffled balance, vertigo
and pink and always finding a mate.
The bird watcher is in the Aleutian
Islands waiting for a good storm
to toss an off-course Asiatic

wing or two his way. His room
a thousand miles downstream is filling
up with so many pictures of feathers
it is starting to come unmoored.
The bird watcher is crawling under

an abandoned trailer in the Midwest
after rumors of a nest clamoring
unkempt worms for the newest
species of red-tailed, blue-bellied
bonnet sparrows, long thought extinct

this side of the Mississippi. The bird
watcher's yard is streamlined viewing
with gullies everywhere and species
wading upstream all the time
right to his window tips, waving

hello or goodbye over the sills
clear into his living room,
down the hallway, past marble
busts, owl, hawk, and tomtit,
up the stairs, and under his skin.

I HAVE TO BEND UNDER
THE YELLOW POLICE TAPES

to go from one room to another.
I have to do a duckwalk
over, among, between the bodies.

It's more annoying every day.
An investigation that never ends.
New evidence always arriving.

My fingerprints are everywhere
but I don't remember a thing.
It's called growing up, I think,

but even I don't believe that.
Mom's lips are pistachio, Dad
has disappeared into his chalk

outline, Sis's blood is drying
into stress wrinkles. The pile
gets higher and higher, Grandpa,

Uncle Albert, Mae, until now
I can't even think of leaving
the house. The good news is

the authorities can't get in
anymore. I was told
to keep a secret diary

but there's nothing
interesting to put in it.
Maybe a post-natal rash,

a reckless case of teen-age
pimples. I stretch out on the bodies
and daydream about getting older.

ABOUT THE AUTHOR

James Doyle grew up in the Bronx. He went to college in
Mexico, and, later, Wisconsin. Upon graduating, he worked
full-time in Wisconsin politics. After returning to school to
study poetry at the Iowa Writers' Workshop, he taught at the
university level in Colorado. He and his wife, poet Sharon
Doyle, live in Fort Collins, Colorado. They are retired, with
lots of time to read, write, and spend with their children and
grandchildren.

www.ingramcontent.com/pod-product-compliance
Lightning Source LLC
Chambersburg PA
CBHW062011040426
42447CB00010B/2003